# God is all around

A Collection of Inspirational Writings and Paintings
Nancy Dunaway McCormick and Marye Ellen Stevens Thomas

GOOD NEWS *Associates*
Seattle, Washington

## In Appreciation

…to GOOD NEWS *Associates*, an organization who encourages "non-traditional" ministry as a way to spread the GOOD NEWS of God's love and grace. GOOD NEWS *Associates* believed in the goodness of the stories in this little book and encouraged it and the accompanying CD into reality.

…to Jan Wood who believes.

…to Boo Boo and her granddaughter Patricia, whose spirit of giving lives on in her.

…to Jonathan Vogel-Borne who devotedly designed the book in the spirit of whimsy. He truly captured the authors' imagination and heart.

…to Nate Macy who listened with his sensitive heart, mind, and ear as he recorded the CD. He was gently supportive as innermost sensitivity was exposed.

…to Chester Friends, a loving group of Quakers, who have nurtured Nancy in developing her gifts as a Minister.

…and most of all—to all those individuals who have suffered strokes, disease, who are going through the dying process, or who are simply resting in their "golden years." You have entrusted intimate moments of your lives and in so doing you have unselfishly taught many lessons. With deep love and respect, both of the authors acknowledge "it is for you this book is written."

**In God's love,
Ellen Thomas and Nancy McCormick**

GOOD NEWS *Associates*
www.goodnewsassoc.org

Copyright © 2006 GOOD NEWS *Associates*

For permission to copy, contact
GOOD NEWS *Associates*
www.goodnewsassoc.org

To contact Nancy McCormick for speaking, retreats, worship music:
www.goodnewsassoc.org

To contact E gallery—Ellen Thomas Art:
102 College Street PO Box 99
Madisonville, Tennessee 37354
(423) 420-1016 | artgallerye@aol.com

McCormick, Nancy Dunaway
Thomas, Marye Ellen
*God is all around*

ISBN 0-9785829-0-X
Inspirational stories, poems and writings with accompanying audio CD.

CD Production: Publishers of Truth,
nate@goodnewsassoc.org

Graphic Design: ASA Graphics,
jvb@theworld.com

Printed by Red Sun Press
Jamaica Plain, MA
redsunpress.com

# Contents

*Elizabeth's Window* – Nancy McCormick, 5

*The Magnetism Of God's Love* – Ellen Thomas, 11

*Just a Hot Soak in the Tub* – Nancy McCormick, 13

*Fireflies* – Nancy McCormick, 17

*Winter Birds* – Ellen Thomas, 19

*Making Fudge* – Nancy McCormick, 21

*Reflections by the Sea* – Nancy McCormick, 25

*"Theologically Sound"* – Ellen Thomas, 27

*Out of Sight Out of Mind* – Nancy McCormick, 29

*We Are Not Supposed to Outlive Our Children* – Nancy McCormick, 33

*A Loving Circle* – Nancy McCormick, 35

*Nanny's Here* – Ellen Thomas, 39

*Shanna's Story* – Nancy and Tallia McCormick, 43

# Elizabeth's Window

**I** WROTE THE FOLLOWING REFLECTION IN **1994** *when I was taking a college course in geriatrics. The couple about whom I wrote have long since passed, however I think of them often and am grateful for the lessons gleaned from them. These were important moments filled with Grace and Light. It was a time of Epiphany, and as I read this now, I know it was a specific time for me—a time to learn. Rendal and Elizabeth helped me understand that we can have glimmers of heaven on earth as we experience "The Eternal Now" (Thomas Kelly,* A Testament of Devotion, *HarperSanFrancisco).*

I am sitting by Elizabeth's window, which is adorned with the colors of autumn and I find myself humming a familiar tune:

> The falling leaves drift by the window
> The autumn leaves of red and gold.
> I see your lips the summer kisses,
> The sunburned hands I use to hold.
> Since you went away the days grow long
> And soon I'll hear old winter's song.
> But I'll miss you most of all my darling
> When autumn leaves start to fall.
> —Jacques Pervert

## God is all around

**T**HIS TUNE BRINGS TO MY MIND A ROMANTIC SETTING IN FRANCE of a lonely lover recalling what was once his. His memories are as brilliant and bold as the splashes of reds and gold strewn amidst a lovers' lane. The lyrics speak of love and lovers and sing of their romance; a romance he does not want to fade away. But people in love are like trees that give us their lustrous leaves. In their season they too grow old.

Sitting here in room 209 of a local nursing home, I see autumn leaves drift by Elizabeth's window. Elizabeth is a woman who cannot acknowledge one's presence with words. I see her gentle 78-year-old husband kiss and stroke her hands. Hands not burned by the sun, but hands that are gnarled and covered by transparent skin, displaying a purple luster. The tune laments on in my mind as this man strokes his wife's forehead and speaks of children, grandchildren, and now a new great-granddaughter. I sense a lump in my throat that feels as if it could burst at any moment if tears are not released. I feel privileged to be in the presence of these two lovers who have embraced a "winter's song." I am sure they have shared summer kisses and held each other's sunburned hands. I am in awe as I see their spirits reach out to

## Elizabeth's Window

one another, as they hope for another chance to see autumn leaves fall.

Visiting this sacred spot came at a very needy time for me. Earlier in the day I received a phone call from a close friend; said she needed to confess, and I was the priest for the day. Her confession was clear and short, although as I listened, I felt as if I had been cut down by enemy fire. "I have had an affair. I am in deep trouble and do not know what to do." I listened to her ramble on nervously, (like a good priest should), allowing her to cleanse herself of the darkness.

As I sat and watched Rendal take great pains to feed Elizabeth, I realized it was my turn to be cleansed. I needed to be assured people really do commit to each other. I needed my doubts and fears washed away by the power of their love. My attention is drawn back to Rendal and Elizabeth. His voice has a droning effect as he continues to urge Elizabeth to eat. With each spoonful, Rendal blows on the steamy pureed food. Still she grimaces with each bite, yet Rendal continues to faithfully feed his mate.

While I sit, watch, and listen, I glance out the window as drifting leaves catch my attention. They seem magical at times the way they sway back and forth almost as if they are suspended in time like the memories within this room. Rendal is having difficulty in getting Elizabeth to eat. As he encourages her, Elizabeth's clear blue eyes are intent on him. I wonder what she is thinking?

## God is all around

The tune of the song continues to haunt me, "since you went away the days grow long." When Rendal comes to see Elizabeth it is always late afternoon, during supper. I wonder if he does this to fill a long lonely gap in his evening—his "winter's song?"

The room in which we are sitting is far from Paris, France. I do not see many young lovers, but I do see people who are very much in love—the kind of love that is devoted to another's soul. Rendal's youngest son says of his parents, "they have the greatest love story going." I cannot think of a better legacy to leave children. Scripture speaks of a time for everything. The seasons also echo this. Winter speaks of silence and cold, a time to prepare the earth before she gives birth to spring. Summer offers time for growth and to nurture what spring has given us. When autumn leaves begin to fall, we are reminded of things slipping from us, never again to return. Although Rendal and Elizabeth are unaware of their gift to me, I feel they have given me the ability to see with different eyes. Thomas Kelly states, "The experience of Now is that of unspeakable and exquisite joy, peace, serene release. A new song is put into our mouths. It is not we who sing; it is the Eternal Song to the Other, who sings in us, who sings unto us, and through us into the world." This room is hallowed. I feel this way because I have seen lovers totally present in their present moment. With this thought in mind, I cannot finish my paper as I intended. It would take the power away from my experience. Perhaps I would

## Elizabeth's Window

have made silly remarks such as "Even the elderly still enjoy kissing" or "Love never grows old." What a waste this would have been. Thomas Kelly goes on to say, "Submit yourself to the Eternal Now, and in peace serene, in the boldness of perfect faith, you can advance into miraculous living."

The chance to sit by Elizabeth's window has offered me much. It has allowed me to see things through her eyes. She, like her window, is quiet, only moving when someone else prompts her. The window, like Elizabeth, silently watches all that passes by. Looking through Elizabeth's window has allowed me to experience people in a different light.

The sun is now setting and we prepare to leave. I step out into the hallway giving this couple time for their holy moment. As we walk down the hall, the only sound I hear is the clicking of our heels. Rendal and I are lost in our own thoughts. The silence is broken as we open the door to leave this part of his world. We both comment on the beauty of the sunset and marvel at its colors. Rendal shuffles along as we make our way to the car. He stops to rest and then looks at me saying, "she looked much better tonight, don't you agree?" I nodded my head making no comment and caught an autumn leaf as it fell.

—*Nancy McCormick*

# The Magnetism Of God's Love

**THANK YOU, O, GOD, FOR THE MAGNETISM OF YOUR LOVE,**
You draw us together even though we are different in so many ways.
You pull our hearts together in a bond of love
If we Let You!

How good You are, blessed Mother/Father
I am filled with gratitude that You are
Inclusive with Your Love,
That no one is excluded,
But instead, You gather each of us
To Your Magnetic Heart Of Love
  —*Ellen Thomas*

# Just a Hot Soak in the Tub

**A**T THE TIME OF THIS WRITING, I AM 50 OR 51 YEARS OLD. I am not sure which! It's not because I do not want people to know my age. I'm simply not a numbers person, and I can't keep up unless I pull my fingers out of my pocket and start doing the math. I do know I am middle aged and tired. It has been a long day, a long week, and a long month; so, why not relax in a nice hot bath to rejuvenate? You know, the kind of bath you read about or see on television or on the theatre screen. The kind where there are a gazillion lit candles, music softly playing, and your head is gently titled back with bubbles up to your chin. As I went about preparing my bath, my time to relax and recharge, my six year-old granddaughter decided to join me.

I knew I was in trouble when she got out three washcloths, a coffee cup, a squirt bottle, a bottle of bubbles and various other items for the bath. I knew I was in trouble when she asked me what size my panties were. Then she asked about my scars, stretch marks, and wrinkles.

## God is all around

Determined to relax, I continued on with my plan and that was to soak in the tub, pretending to be in a far away place. Suddenly, the water came squirting at me from every direction and hitting me in precarious places with such force that I began to giggle. I could not stop! Hilarious laughter poured out of me, I howled so much my whole body shook, and I do mean—SHOOK! During this frivolity my granddaughter looked at me and said, "Grammy, I love it when your belly shakes!" Her statement brought me back to reality and ended any chance of having "just a hot soak in the tub." I lathered up, rinsed off, patted dry, put on my long flannel nightie, and returned to the task at hand, which was taking care of our granddaughter.

### For your consideration

Our granddaughter is here tonight, as she is every night, because her single mother is working. Do you know anyone who is single and raising children alone? It is not an easy job! If you are looking for a way to help someone out, have you thought of assisting a one-parent family? You could help by inviting them to dinner or perhaps dropping off some goodies to their home. It's a tough job raising children even when there are two

## Just a Hot Soak in the Tub

parents. Not every single parent has the luxury of having loving grandparents who care for their child/children as does our daughter. Many people live miles away from any family. Take the opportunity to get to know the single parent with whom you work, or who lives in your neighborhood, or with whom you worship. Reach out to them. Your life will be blessed as well as changed, and adopted families are sometimes just what the doctor ordered!

In the meantime, do you know people who are babysitting their grandchildren? Call them and offer to take the kids for a while, so Grammy can take a "hot soak in the tub" while Pa scrubs her back.

—Nancy McCormick

# Fireflies

*"O Lord our Lord, how majestic is your name in all the earth!"* —Psalm 8:9

**W**HY DID GOD MAKE FIREFLIES? Was the Creator inspired to make critters that fly and shine while sitting by a babbling brook? Was moon glow not yet invented, were paths still dim, when God determined to release these shimmering rays? Were fireflies formed to be the original lightning bolts but were too timid to bellow and roar? Have you given it much thought or are you shaking your head saying, "WHO CARES?"

As a parent I could not wait until my children were old enough to chase those magical creatures of light. I recall the time we invited company to our home solely to watch fireflies and we oohed and aahed as they floated by.

Let the God who created such mystical creatures as the fireflies renew within us the childlike ability to SEE the Wonders of Creation. Let God remind us of the things we tend to forget about as we age. Did you ever catch a tree frog and giggle with delight? Did you ever wonder why a bullfrog croaks at night? Think about tiny horses that live in the sea! And what about the hummingbird? Listen to her song as she zooms by your head. Look at her carefully and know The Great One spun her with golden threads. Don't be afraid to reunite with that inner childhood friend. Renew your spirit and let your heart rejoice.

1. What are the marvels of God's creation that bring you into God's presence?
2. Do you have a childhood memory to share?
3. Why do you think fireflies were created?

—Nancy McCormick

# Winter Birds

**HOW BEAUTIFUL ARE THE VARIED BIRDS**
Flying all about!
Swooping up, diving down,
Plucking seeds I've scattered out.

How curious for me to note –
As I watch a mourning dove –
Birds feeding on the ground below,
Draw my heart to God above.
—Ellen Thomas

**Bird Feeders**
*1 package plain sliced bagels
1 jar peanut butter, plain or crunchy
1 bag birdseed
string, ribbon, or twine*

*Separate bagels and dry until hard. Spread peanut butter on bagel slices and roll in bird seed. Tie with ribbon or string.*

This reflection is about a little girl I met while I was working on my social work degree in Belize, Central America. This child stirred something deep within me, reminding me of the sacredness of doing the smallest of tasks. It is my desire through this journal entry that you will be reminded of God's presence as you go about your daily rounds.

# Making Fudge

**G**UADALUPE CAME BY THE HOUSE TODAY. Her school was having a carnival and the children were asked to bring homemade fudge to sell to raise money. I cringed because I instinctively knew what her next comment was going to be, "Miss Nancy, will you help me make some fudge to take to the carnival?" I muttered to myself, anything but fudge God; a candy maker I am not! It's a fact. In all the years I have been cooking, I have made only one decent batch of fudge. Guadalupe had an incredible power of persuasion, and I found myself gathering my pocket book as we went out the door to the market. Lupae was confident that this would be the grandest fudge in all of Belize! Oh Lord, I mumbled, the pressure is on! Of course, I could find nothing in the kitchen with which to work, so everything was measured by guess and by golly. I looked at Lupae with pleading in my eyes and pain in my heart. She patted me, assuring me this fudge would not come between us. We cooked and we stirred following the procedures to the letter. I was beginning to feel confident as the aroma wafted about and fudge splattered all over me. We poured that candy in several pans, put it in the refrigerator to harden; and then sat down in great anticipation… waiting, waiting, waiting.

To make time move more quickly, we set about doing some homework. I drilled Lupae on spelling words and helped her

## God is all around

read and re-read several stories. I noticed she was becoming fidgety. Thinking it was because of our candy project, I assured her the fudge would soon be done, but she stated she was not worried about the fudge. Lupae then began talking like an adult instead of a seven year-old child. She said her mommy wanted to borrow sixty dollars to pay their rent and then she quickly looked away. I was shocked and my heart was broken, not because she asked for money but because this little child was asked to do what a grown up should have done. Lupae could tell I was disturbed and she began to sob.

"God, help me find healing words, because I do not know what to say." I prayed. I sat quietly and held Lupae, stroking her head while I thought. It became clear to me that I simply needed to speak truth. Lupae was mature for her age and would understand. "Lupae, I do not know if I can loan your mommy the money, but I do know this; if I decide I cannot do it, that does not mean you were a bad girl for asking me. Nothing will come in the way of our friendship. I also think it must be awfully hard on a seven year-old to make such grownup decisions." After saying this, Miss Lupae melted into my lap and sobbed. We both sobbed. I then let her know she was a strong and courageous girl.

Well, that fudge never did set. I considered it to be a big flop, but Guadalupe looked at me with great delight as we worked together wrapping individual messy pieces in Saran Wrap. Guadalupe carried her fudge to the carnival that evening with great pride knowing that nothing would come between us, not even a bad case of fudge.

## Making Fudge

**GOD, IT HAS BEEN A LONG WHILE SINCE I HAVE SEEN GUADALUPE.**
My heart aches when I think about all the things
that could go wrong in her life. I have tried many times to
reconnect with her when I travel back to Belize.
I pray one day when she sees a piece of fudge she will remember
the bond that was made between us as we stirred and giggled over
chocolaty syrup. May we both continue to work and live in your
peace as we experience your Light and Love. Amen
—*Nancy McCormick*

# Mom's Fudge Recipe

½ can evaporated milk  
½ c. butter  
16 large marshmallows (cut up)  
2½ c. of sugar  
12 oz. chocolate chips  
1 tsp. vanilla

Mix all the above together in a saucepan. When it begins to boil, stir and time for 5 min. Stir throughout. Turn temperature down, but continue to boil. After 5 min. take off heat and add 12 oz chocolate chips and 1 tsp. vanilla. Stir, then pour in greased pan.

P.S. Mom says if you boil more than 5 min. it will get hard as a rock!

*During my time in Belize City, Central America, I went daily to the sea wall for spiritual and physical renewal. The following poem is an entry in my journal about how God renewed and refreshed me while sitting by the sea.*

# Reflections By The Sea

AS I SIT BY THE SEA
I am reminded of the healing power of God
I feel I am sitting in the womb of God.
The sea is ever rumbling and roaring with the Gift Of Life.
It is a place where I have rediscovered God's goodness and incredible Light –
Light that has helped me be at peace with the incredible me.
Shhhush, be quiet now and watch the Light dance and radiate, illuminating each wave.
The color bounces from the depths below, sparkling and bringing new life from within.
Come and sit by her side.
Sit and listen and let her goodness inspire you.
Let her waves caress and hold your tired and weary soul.
You will find strength –
Incredible strength –
To do those things you never dreamed of
To rediscover dreams that have long since washed ashore.
Let her cool refreshment splash upon your face,
Reminding you of God's cool streams
As they await you in your desert place.
When you have emerged in this Ocean Of Love you will rediscover
The Power—The Awesome Power—Of God's Grace.

1. The author of this poem found renewal by the sea, where do you go for renewal?
2. How is the character of God represented in nature?
3. What does the phrase "emerged in the Ocean of Love" mean to you?

—Nancy McCormick

# "Theologically Sound"

GOD IN HEAVEN AND IN OUR HEARTS –
Thank you that we don't have to be "theologically sound"
To receive Your tender mercies,
I'm glad You don't go over a checklist of doctrinal requirements
Each time You extend Your comfort.
You made us and You know of our Humanity –
Of our smallness of mind –
Of our smallness of belief –
And yet You come to us in our times of need!
Thank you for the peace and hope with which You continue
To bless Your children.
Shalom

—Ellen Thomas

# Out of Sight Out of Mind

**THE OLD ADAGE "OUT OF SIGHT OUT OF MIND" IS A REALITY FOR MANY FOLK.** One of the things I have learned while working with the elderly is their fear of being forgotten by their friends, their church and their family as their lives slow down. Recently I visited a resident who was adjusting to her new surroundings. She began to speak of her fears of losing her usefulness and her value to others. "What good am I in this condition? I just don't get around like I used to." She then went on to state one of her deepest concerns; "if I quit driving and the cold weather keeps me from getting out, I will soon be forgotten; you know, 'out of sight out of mind.' You'll see they will quickly forget me." I reassured her she was not the kind of person who could be easily forgotten. She brought many gifts to her corner of the world. She had a great sense of humor. Her heart was full of compassion. She was full of wisdom and had an excellent ear for listening. I also reminded her it takes time when you move and begin anew, and she would soon be meeting many people as she became established in her new home.

## God is all around

I offered her the Spirit of Presence for the remainder of our visit. I sat and listened as she shared what was on her heart and mind. We prayed together thanking God for a full life and asking the Holy One for the courage to endure and face whatever comes along, even if that includes being forgotten.

I left that afternoon feeling sad and unsure of myself because of the reality of, "out of sight out of mind." Could this happen to me some day? Will I be forgotten? Our elderly often are forgotten because they are no longer perceived as productive citizens. What an offense we commit when we do not listen to the life stories from our aged. We fail to glean from them incredible lessons. We are given the opportunity to grow into ourselves as we listen to the wisdom learned from their past mistakes. We can also benefit as we hear accounts of their accomplishments and successes. We reinforce their value when we ask to hear their tales of long ago… tales that disclose powerful recollections revealing buried treasure.

1. Has there been a time in your life when you have felt forgotten?
2. Do you ask to hear the life stories of the shut-ins and elderly in your community?
3. How can you tell your own life story?

—*Nancy McCormick*

## Out of Sight Out of Mind

# We Are Not Supposed To Outlive Our Children, Are We?

**I** WAS DEEPLY MOVED AS I WALKED INTO ALICE'S ROOM. Her grief was evidenced by the way my elderly friend sat. It was as if her soul had left her body. Alice is not supposed to be this way; it is she who is strong. It is she who brings comfort to others. Today her face was vacant, yet full of pain. Her body was rigid yet limp as a willow. She melted into my arms, as I embraced her, quietly she sobbed, "how can this be, he was alive two days ago. We are not supposed to outlive our children are we?" What a shock it had been for her to hear the news of her son's sudden death. I listened to the few things she had to say. The rest of the time was spent holding one another in Silence, honoring that Sacred Place, a place of deep pain. At times like this I am reminded Silence is truly a gift. We do not need to feel awkward when Silence comes, nor do we need to fill it with words. We simply need to embrace it…

1. Why are we afraid of Silence?
2. Can you name a time Silence has been your friend?
3. Why is the gift of touch so important?

—Nancy McCormick

# A Loving Circle

**I**T IS DIFFICULT TO LOAD A CAR FULL OF ELDERLY WOMEN. The seat belts are mechanically challenging, finding room for their walkers is a great engineering feat, and temperature control is a driver's nightmare. But when that load of women is on a mission, it is worth the effort. Our mission on this particular Wednesday was to visit a friend in the local nursing home. She had broken her hip, had it surgically repaired and was now recovering. I hope I never forget the look on Kathleen's face as we entered her room. She could not believe so many of her friends had come to visit her. Kathleen had made many visits to the sick before her accident. On these visits she often took a chocolate bar to help cheer the mood.

## God is all around

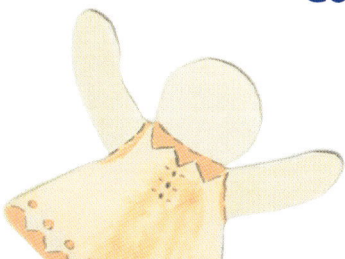

Now it was our turn to cheer her. We gathered around her bed with our chairs, canes and walkers and began our visit. On that morning, this circle of women did what women do best when we are open to God's spirit—we simply loved her. We sang, laughed, shared stories, and prayed, as The Sacred was at hand. As our visit came to a close, each person approached Kathleen to say goodbye in her own unique way—some with a kiss, hug or gentle caress. We then walked out of her room, slowly and deliberately. It was almost symbolic of the many who had wandered in and out of Kathleen's life over the years. We had come to bring Christ's peace to our friend. We left with our hearts encouraged, we left experiencing God's love.

A week later Kathleen was struggling in the Critical Care Unit of Clinton Memorial Hospital. She spoke of places and people who were long gone. As I stood in the Silence and stroked her head, I recalled the circle of women who had recently blessed her with their gift of love. Unsure of what to say, I simply prayed the circle of love from our previous visit would be the gift to carry her through…

## A Loving Circle

1. Can you share from your own experiences of being in a loving circle?
2. What are some obstacles you face when trying to visit a sick friend?
3. What are some other ways in which Kathleen could have been ministered to?

—*Nancy McCormick*

# Nanny's Here

**T**HE OCCASION WAS MY GRANDNIECE HANNAH'S CHRISTENING. My sisters and I were scurrying about the church fellowship hall preparing for the luncheon following the service. My sister Barbara, Hannah's Grandmother, brought tablecloths, buckets of spring flowers, serving pieces, and other items to make the hall festive. I brought an assortment of milk glass bud vases our mother ("Nanny" to her grandchildren) had collected to fill with flowers. My sister Elizabeth was busy arranging tables and putting things in order to efficiently serve the guests. Hannah's cousin Clara was helping arrange flowers as her mother decorated each table with the lush spring bouquets. It was a happy time—women bustling about making a life event special as we came together supporting one another with love. It did not matter that Christening was not a part of the spiritual tradition for some of us—it only mattered that we cared enough to make this a special time for Hannah's parents. This is part of the lesson Jesus was teaching in the Scripture passage (John 2: 1–10) where he turned the water into wine at the wedding feast. He joyfully contributed to the happy event. He let kindness and concern shine through instead of quibbling over religious ritual. This powerful message teaches us about honoring others—regardless of their beliefs as we simply love one another.

"…and he said to them, draw out now, and bear unto the Governor of the feast. And they bear it. When the ruler of the feast had tasted the water that was made wine, and knew not whence it was; (but the servant which drew the water KNEW)…" John 2: 1–10

## God is all around

**SWEET HANNAH, THERE'S SOMETHING**
You should know
About your Christening Day –
Those Springtime flowers
In each bud vase
Had something special to say …

Those vases –
Each and every one –
Were your Great Nanny's
From her collection
Of things of beauty she had added
To those things she called "precious."

Your Great Aunts and Grandmother
Filled those vases and placed them all around
To fill the room with beauty,
To make joy abound!
To gladden hearts and Fill our souls
With happiness and cheer –
But, most of all, to whisper close,
"Dear Hannah – Nanny's Here!"

## Nanny's Here

**Things to Ponder:**
- —Have religious differences prevented you from participating or supporting someone in Special Life Events?
- —How can I celebrate events / rituals that strengthen the truth of God's unconditional love?
- —Am I sensitive to God's leadings regarding…[fill in the blank]?

—Ellen Thomas

Nanny's Punch
2 cans frozen white grape juice concentrate
2 cans frozen apple juice concentrate
2 "frozen juice cans" water
2 2 liter bottles ginger ale
Combine and serve ice cold—

# God Moments – Shanna's Story

**I**N ORDER TO DISCOVER GOD MOMENT'S IN OUR LIVES, we need to sit, listen, watch, and learn from others. In the scriptures we read of Jesus sitting with the children. Too many times we dismiss little ones because as we grow older we forget the great pleasure that comes to us as we play and use our imagination. Many people think one needs to be "Holier Than Thou" to be Godly, soon forgetting how to laugh and interact with one another. I am learning that God Moments can come in many different ways—laughing, playing, dancing, singing, eating, painting, writing, kissing, praying, holding hands, watching animals, listening to birds, tickling children, saying I am sorry, riding horses, raking leaves, visiting a neighbor, baking cookies for an inmate, sewing lap blankets for the elderly. God Moments come in all kinds of ways. Forgive us, God, for teaching or pretending they don't.

I am grateful for God Moments.
Playing with my granddaughter enables me to experience
these Moments as I am drawn by her spirit into the presence of
God's Love, Joy and Peace.

*(The following tale developed as my granddaughter and I were playing "let's make up a story.")*

**God is all around**

# Shanna's Family

Once upon a time there was a little girl
by the name of Tallia Rose.
Because Tallia is using her imagination
She will be called Shanna in this story.

Shanna lived with her mommy, Tess. Shanna's mommy worked at night at the Pub, so she stayed with her Grammy and Pa in the evenings. At the time of this unusual story, Shanna is 5 years old, (for real).

Shanna likes her family very much, but her family lived in many different places. In Shanna's imagination she wanted her family to live close by. In this story they all live together in the Quaker Meeting House near Wilmington, Ohio. Aunt Betsy, Cousin Steve, Uncle Dave, Cousin Lisa, Shanna's mom, her Aunt Jenny, baby Ben, Aunt Cynthia, Grandma Gee Gee, Pa and Grammy, and Mary Huffman (a friend of the family).

The first decision that needed to be made was who is going to cook for all of these people? Shanna decided she would go first, because she wanted to be the imaginary mother. She invented a scrumptious meal of pancakes, eggs, and bacon. She fixed it on the stove in the basement all by herself. As an addition, Shanna decided to serve peach lemonade to compliment her breakfast. Cousin Steve then decided he did not want any eggs, but Shanna decided she was the boss of the meal and told him he had to eat it all! Then her Great Aunt Betsy and Great Aunt Cynthia and Cousin Lisa decided they did not like the bacon and bread, but Shanna decided they had better eat it all because they needed more calcium in their diet!

## God Moments – Shanna's Story

After breakfast was eaten, Shanna looked around and asked, "Who is going to clean up the mess?" No one answered. So Shanna decided she would do it since she was the mother of the day. She also decided she would be the mother each and every day, because Aunt Betsy said she did not want to be the mother any more—it was just too hard!

Shanna was getting a little nervous with everyone underfoot, so she told Lisa to fetch some eggs. Steve could go milk the cow. Her Great Aunt Cynthia and Great Aunt Betsy and Grandma Gee Gee could start baking some chocolate chip cookies. Mary Huffman could mend some of Pa's britches, and her mommy and Aunt Jenny could vacuum and dust the basement. Pa could tend to the horses and Grammy could help prepare the noon meal.

While they were preparing the meal, Shanna heard Grandma Gee Gee moaning. She quickly went over to Gee Gee and took her temperature. Shanna decided very quickly they needed to take Gee Gee to the hospital, but there were no doctors or nurses when they arrived. So Shanna decided she would be the Doctor for the day and Cousin Lisa would be the nurse. They decided they should give Gee Gee some pills and water. Lisa checked her heart while Shanna looked in her ears. It was in Gee Gee's ears that Shanna discovered the problem! A little tree frog was snuggled up—right smack dab in Gee Gee's

### God is all around

left ear. Shanna had heard of potatoes growing in people's ears but never a frog. She quickly grabbed it as she explained to the little creature that Gee Gee's ear was not the place for a frog. She and Lisa decided to take the little frog outside where they placed it near the fishpond under a pile of leaves. Shanna put her hand in her pocket where she discovered a vegetable seed. Gently she placed the seed on the frog. Immediately a big old carrot grew from the top of the little frog's head. Shanna thought this was marvelous and decided the little frog should come home with them. She could keep it warm in the basement and she would use the carrot for supper!

### God Moments – Shanna's Story

Well, Grandma Gee Gee got better right away. To celebrate, they all went home and ate warm chocolate chip cookies and drank fresh cows' milk. Then Pa hooked up the team of horses and gave everyone a wagon ride as they happily ate homemade ice cream.

—*Nancy and Tallia McCormick*

## God is all around

**THIS ENDS THE STORY OF SHANNA AND HER FAMILY.**

*Dear God, I am grateful for those God Moments
of holding babies while I sing.
I am grateful for the time I heard 'Holy' giggles as children played.
I am grateful for people you have brought my way,
teaching me not to be too serious—reminding me that 'Holy Living' can be
done in an attitude of play. I am grateful for the wonder of
Your Creation—did You sit in utter delight as you designed incredible creatures? Did you
play with them before you let them go?
I believe so….I truly believe so.*

**What are some God Moments you have experienced in your life?**